The Art of
Disney
ENCANTO

The Art of Disney

Encanto

CHRONICLE BOOKS

SAN FRANCISCO

This book includes depictions of artwork of the Zenú, Aguadas, and La Chamba communities. Mirabel's bag was inspired by the Mochila from the Wayuu community.

Creating a computer-generated animated film involves years of inspired collaboration. Before the final rendered images of *Encanto* were seen on screens around the world, the following artists contributed their talents to the images included in this book:

Alberto Abril, Shaun Absher, Theresa Adolph, Chris Anderson, Joaquin Baldwin, Ksenia Bezrukov, Nicholas Burkard, Sergi Caballer, Ramya Chidanand, Jennifer Downs, Colin Eckart, Jim Finn, Leticia Gillet, Richard Gouge, Eric Hansen, David Hutchins, Katherine Ipjian, Jay Jackson, Alessandro Jacomini, Tammy Kersavage, SuZan Kim, Ian Krebs-Smith, Luis Labrador, Todd LaPlante, Brandon Lawless, Suki Lee, Richard Lehmann, Jonathan Lin, Eric Mclean, Michael A. Navarro, Chris O'Connell, Chris Pedersen, Joseph Piercy, Nicklas Puetz, Daniel Rice, Ryan Rogers, Rissa Sanchez, James Schauf, Benson Shum, Mitchell Snary, Jonathan Soto, Suan Tan, Ryan Tottle, Mary Twohig, Richard Van Cleave, Jose Luis "Weecho" Velasquez, Nathan Warner, Alexander Whang, Elizabeth Willy, and Xinmin Zhao.

Library of Congress Cataloging-in-Publication Data:

Names: Disney Enterprises (1996-), author. | Lee, Jennifer (Screenwriter),
    writer of preface. | Bush, Jared, 1974- writer of foreword. | Howard,
    Byron, writer of foreword. | Castro Smith, Charise, writer of foreword.
Title: The art of Encanto / Disney Enterprises, Inc.
Description: San Francisco : Chronicle Books, [2022]
Identifiers: LCCN 2021042354 | ISBN 9781797200866 (hardcover)
Subjects: LCSH: Encanto (Motion picture) | Animated films–United States.
Classification: LCC NC1766.U53 E533 2022 | DDC 791.43/72–dc23
LC record available at https://lccn.loc.gov/2021042354
Manufactured in Italy.

Design by Jon Glick.

(Cover) **Lorelay Bové** / Digital
(Case): **Neysa Bové** / Digital
(Front Flap) **Bill Schwab** / Digital
(Endsheets) **Neysa Bové** / Digital
(Page 2-3) **Ian Gooding** / Digital
(This Page) **Scott Watanabe** / Digital

10 9 8 7 6 5 4 3

Chronicle Books LLC
680 Second Street
San Francisco, California 94107
www.chroniclebooks.com

Contents

Preface

At Walt Disney Animation Studios, we aspire to create stories of hope—stories that connect us all. In *Encanto*, Byron Howard, Jared Bush, Charise Castro Smith, and Lin-Manuel Miranda tell the story of Mirabel, a girl who on the surface may lack the magical powers of her family members but is imbued with determination and love of family. She'll need those two gifts as she strives to save them and the world as she knows it. What could be more inspiring and universal than that?

Bringing a character like Mirabel into the world is so exciting for the whole Walt Disney Animation Studios team. While Disney Animation has celebrated Latin American cultures and stories in the past, this film marks the first time a Latina heroine is at the fore. She's also a wonderful addition to a long line of ever-evolving, ever-inspiring Disney heroines. She's smart, daring, and strong; she's funny, relatable, and proudly wears glasses (something many of us bespectacled folk can appreciate).

This universal story of family takes its inspiration from the concept of magical realism and the beautiful cultures in Colombia. The filmmakers were deeply touched by their research trip there, and that admiration and respect carried through the making of the film as they continued to work with cultural experts from the region.

The stunning visuals, emotional story, and incredible music within this film are a reflection of the deep love that each and every person on the filmmaking team felt. It is a pleasure to be a part of a community that has crafted a story as vibrant, original, and inspiring as *Encanto*. This book shares a selection of the incredible artwork created for the film by some of the best visual artists in the world, as well as gives a peek behind the curtain into the filmmakers' creative process. Please enjoy.

Jennifer Lee

Foreword

Hace mucho tiempo . . . a long time ago . . . we embarked on the journey of *Encanto*. We didn't know who our characters might be, we didn't know how our story would unfold, we only knew that we wanted our movie to be about family . . . and so the joy and pain began.

How well do we know our families? How well do our families know us? These are the questions we asked as we set out in search of a story, and it wasn't long before we made three important discoveries: 1) *most* of us don't feel truly seen by our families, 2) *most* of us carry burdens we never let our families see, and 3) *most* of us are oblivious that nearly *all of us*, especially within our own families, feel the exact same way. We had our story.

From the beginning, we knew music would play a big part in our movie. We knew this, because Lin-Manuel Miranda was our creative partner from day one. The more we all talked, the more excited we became to tell a story about family through song; letting the music of each character speak to universal truths and shared experiences. But what would it sound like? Which rhythms would best capture the syncopation of siblings and parents and cousins? Right away, Lin-Manuel knew the vibrant, broad spectrum of the music of Latin America would bring our family story to life.

We dove in immediately, connecting our themes of family and perspective with the music and cultures of Latin America, keeping our eyes open for a setting that would encapsulate it all. Together, with the help of our Familia, a group of Disney artists, technicians, staff, friends and family, we were drawn to Colombia,

often considered the crossroads of Latin America—a melting pot of Latin culture, music, dance, art, and food, with some of the greatest biodiversity on the planet. So we packed our bags and a group of us, including Lin-Manuel and his dad, Luis, set out to experience Colombia for ourselves. Without question, our time in Colombia was life-changing and deeply inspiring and above all else, filled us with a passion to celebrate the people we met, the friends we made, and the families who welcomed us into their homes. There was music, there was food . . . and there was magic.

Colombia is often thought of as the home of magical realism. And while we always say *Encanto* is not *true* magical realism, it is absolutely inspired by the great literary traditions of writers like Gabriel García Márquez, Isabel Allende, and Jorge Luis Borges, among many others. Their stories aren't fantasy, but reality as told through a unique lens: heightened moments and emotions combined to invoke a feeling, to explain a complicated world, to deal with a painful past. Some of these moments are spectacular . . . while many others are treated as commonplace. To tell the story of *Encanto*, we immersed ourselves and tried to learn from the greats, both past and present.

The most elusive question left to answer, even as of the writing of this book, was: What would this movie look like? How would we translate these ideas, this world, these characters, this family, to the screen? Well, our answer was simple: assemble the very best artists, and animators, and lighters, and engineers, and cinematographers, and effects geniuses, and storytellers, and consultants, and actors, and choreographers, and musicians, and producers, and production staff on the planet. Their unbridled creativity, their unique perspectives, their unwavering care, and their own

families' stories are what you will find in every image that follows.

Within these pages we wanted to celebrate our journey. We wanted to share our process, to show how a kernel of an idea can spark a character, how a sketch can bloom into song, how one image can unlock an entire world. Ours is not a linear filmmaking process, we don't see the finish line until we've crossed it. The best idea one day, is in the garbage the next . . . and sometimes, three years later, it crawls its way out of the dumpster and becomes the missing piece we never knew we needed. Or not. But in one way or another, we are all putting ourselves on the page, we are drawing our lives on the screen. We are opening up and sharing who we are, and for a film about perspective, we needed as many points of view, as many different experiences as possible. We were so lucky to have a crew, a community, a family that cared enough to let us see the world through their eyes.

Five years is a long time. 2016 to 2021 felt like a century. Never did we think we would make a movie about a home, from our actual homes. Never did we think we'd see such a need for perspective in a world so unable to see beyond its own limited view. But like a family, we grew up together during the making of this movie. Babies were born, loved ones were lost. We laughed together, we fought with each other, we shed tears of happiness and sorrow, we helped one another, we tried to hear each other, and ultimately, like with every family, we probably all remember it a little differently.

The Madrigal family was blessed with a miracle. The family who created *Encanto,* was ours.

Jared Bush, Byron Howard, Charise Castro Smith

Meg Park / Digital

IT TAKES A FAMILY TO MAKE A FAMILY

THIS SPREAD: **Byron Howard** / Digital

A Family of Inspiration

"OUR BELOVED COLOMBIA IS KNOWN AS a crossroad of cultures, a place with people of Indigenous, African, and European descent. Latin America is so diverse but sadly often homogenized in the media. By setting a film of this magnitude there, you have the opportunity to show all the cultural and natural richness of our country." That was the biggest wish made by Juan Rendon and Natalie Osma, the Colombian filmmakers and producers that Byron Howard and Jared Bush met while making a documentary about their previous film together, *Zootopia*.

Howard and Bush had recently gone back into development on their next film together, and were

Byron Howard and Jared Bush

excited to collaborate with Lin-Manuel Miranda to make Walt Disney Animation Studios' take on a Latin American musical. Together with consultants including Rendon and Osma, they embarked on a journey of discovery to learn more about Colombia and how best to reflect the country's culture and environments on the big screen.

After thoroughly exploring the local resources near Disney's Burbank studio, Howard and Bush set off to Colombia to see and feel the culture for themselves. "You have to experience the different regions

Photographs by **Jared Bush**, **Bryan Davidson**, and **Byron Howard**

of our country because each one is so different," say Rendon and Osma, who accompanied the filmmakers for portions of the trip. "Colombia can be divided into five completely different regions: the Caribbean and Pacific coasts, the Andes mountain range, the plains, and the Amazon rainforest. It was important to show that range in the film." In pursuit of this goal, the filmmakers traveled to grand cities such as Bogotá and Cartagena, to endearing small towns like Barichara, Salento, and Palenque, and stunning natural landmarks like the Cocora Valley.

Along the way, they met local Colombians and engaged in extended conversations about what they would like to see in a film like this. One particular highlight was their Barichara tour guide, Alejandra Espinosa, who also happens to be a published author and Colombian culture aficionado. "You have it all wrong!" she told them, after the filmmakers had shown her early sketches of their family story where the father was the central figure. "You can't tell the story of a patriarchy in Colombia; women are in charge here."

Lin-Manuel and his father Luis Miranda, a longtime advocate for the Latin American community, also joined Howard and Bush on the trip. A standout musical moment for the team was with a group of people playing their traditional drums in Palenque, a

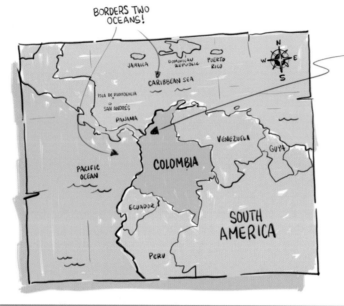

COLOMBIA!

BORDERS TWO OCEANS!

"GATEWAY TO SOUTH AMERICA"

MELTING POT OF INFLUENCES

INDIGENOUS · SPANISH · AFRICAN

BOTH

CULTURAL & MUSICAL

Jason Hand / Digital

place known for its population of African descent and for being the first "free town" of the Americas. In Barichara they joined a session of traditional Colombian tiple guitar players, which Howard enjoyed so much that he immediately bought a tiple of his own.

After the trip was over, the work continued, and the people of Colombia remained a consistent part of the film's development. Professor of plant biology Felipe Zapata met with the team to discuss the variety of Colombian orchids and the many different rainforests of the region; architects Stefano and Martin Anzellini and Maria Inés Garcia-Reyes explained the structure of Colombian towns and houses; anthropologists Andrés Góngora and Sara Zamora shared traditional regional costumes and symbology; and Edna Liliana Valencia Murillo, journalist and activist, helped in the authentic representation of the film's Afro-Colombian characters like Félix, Antonio, Camilo, and Dolores.

While this immersion and education was important to shaping the look and feel of *Encanto*'s homage to Colombia, it also brought a new energy to the emotional heart of the story: the importance of family. "I come from a very big extended Italian family," says Howard, "and I had always wanted to tell a story about that experience."

Juan Rendon and Natalie Osma

Alejandra Espinosa

from Byron and Jared to do this project was such an unexpected and amazing gift," says Castro Smith. "The potential of this film was so moving to me, mainly because of the characters we were representing. The idea of putting people that are not often represented up on screen for the world to see just felt momentous. It wasn't even a question of if I wanted to be a part of it; I had to be a part of it."

Once Producers Clark Spencer and Yvett Merino joined, the core team was complete. This cross-section of inspiration close to home and the richness of Colombia's culture and people continued to set the tone for *Encanto*. As the film moved into design and production, the love of family and Colombia always remained at its core.

In exploring the family dynamic and themes at the core of their film, Bush also looked to his own family history: "My older sister and I were talking about growing up, and I described how supportive my parents were of me following my Hollywood dreams. I was shocked when she shared that her experience was quite different—that she had always felt pressured by our parents into excelling at gymnastics instead of exploring other interests she loved. We just had very different perspectives, and we had never shared them." Prompted by this discovery, Bush shaped the story of *Encanto* around the complexity of perspective within a family, and the very human feeling of not being heard by the ones who love us most—a feeling reflected in the film's leading character, Mirabel.

As the film was finding its heroine in Mirabel, Howard and Bush also found a new partner to help them tell the story, Co-Writer and Co-Director Charise Castro Smith. "For me, getting the call

Photographs by **Byron Howard** and **Jared Bush**

Byron Howard / Digital

By age four he had grown a moustache
by the sheer force of his will.

By his twenties, the moustache
was resplendent.

He was warned by
a mysterious woman not to
build a house there.

On the first night in his home, it was clear to Agustín
that he, as always, had acted wisely.

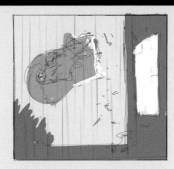

The house did not agree.

Each child in turn discovered that they
had been given a special talent.

"Early on we explored many different versions of what the story could be, even before the character of Mirabel was born. In one version, we had a young woman receive a magical doorknob, transporting her to an unexpected world. In a different version, Agustín was a patriarch who found the Encanto where he builds the magical home."—Byron Howard, Director

A Family of Collaboration

Familia Group

Byron Howard / Digital

IN THE EARLY DAYS OF THE WALT DISNEY Animation Studios, Walt Disney himself outlined the concept of "plussing": that every project can be improved upon by each hand that touches it. *Encanto* was no exception in applying this principle, taking the Studio's collaborative nature to heart.

Since the very beginning of the story's development, Byron Howard and Jared Bush looked to the Studio's Latina and Latino employees to bring personal and authentic narratives to their film, forming the "Familia" group. Not only did this group inspire the early core of the film, but they stayed connected throughout development and production, sharing personal stories, giving input on the film, and even throwing their own holiday parties together. Similarly, our Walt Disney Animation Studios' Black Employees group was with us on the journey for the portrayal of our Afro-Colombian characters.

As the story progressed, Howard, Bush, and Castro Smith set the collaborative tone at every team meeting by welcoming as many perspectives as they could into the film's dedicated story room. "From early on, the art and story teams were invited by the directors to be in the room for each other's meetings, allowing for a lot more cross-pollination between departments," Heads of Story Jason Hand and Nancy Kruse recall. "This way, for example, a visual development artist could be inspired by panels drawn by a story artist and create a painting or design to support that idea," adds Meg Park, a visual development artist.

"I wanted to carry on that collaborative spirit established by the directors as part of the process for our art team," says Production Designer Ian Gooding, "so I would invite both character and environment artists to see each other's work during regular

Bill Schwab / Digital

Meg Park / Digital

meetings. This allowed everyone to be on the same page and create a cohesive aesthetic."

This philosophy was also a big part of the character design process, as Art Director for Characters Bill Schwab outlines: "For this particular film, the directors wouldn't have one individual person focus on each character, but would instead assign the same character to different people all at once. Then, we would share our designs with each other, allowing room to play and discover what everyone brought from their own unique point of view."

Meg Park / Digital

James Woods / Digital

Every department continued this collaborative and additive process down the pipeline to the finished film. "At the end of the day, the goal for each one of us is to make the next department's job easier," says Character Look Development Artist Jose Luis "Weecho" Velasquez, "and if that's the case, we know we did our part."

Gabriel

Raimi

Princesa

THIS SPREAD: Lorelay Bové / Digital

Alejandra

Miranda

Pepa y Leta

Agustín

THIS SPREAD: **Lorelay Bové** / Digital

"When we did these early designs, the film took place in the 1950s and had a more global look. It later shifted to having a 1900s feel, a folkloric Colombian aesthetic. You can see this shift through many designs in the book. It was fun to get to visually find each character as the directors kept introducing them to me early on, when the story was still so malleable." —Lorelay Bové, Associate Production Designer

Isabella

Hugo

Beatriz

Exploration of Magical Gifts

Jason Hand / Digital

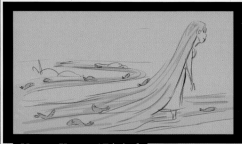

Nancy Kruse / Digital

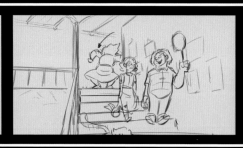
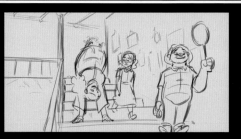

Nancy Kruse / Digital

Mark Kennedy / Digital

"We spent a lot of time brainstorming gifts for the Madrigals in terms of emotion, magical realism, personality, and family roles. We had different artists just let loose and come up with ideas to pitch, and there are so many fun ones shown here that didn't make it into the final film." —Nancy Kruse, Head of Story

Seth Boyden / Digital

Ryan Green / Digital

Tom Ellery / Digital

Mark Kennedy / Digital

Hillary Bradfield / Digital

Samantha Vilfort / Digital

Samantha Vilfort / Digital

Character-Driven Storytelling

SINCE THE VERY FIRST ART TEAM MEETINGS, it was clear that the focus of *Encanto* was going to be on the characters. After all, a family is what turns a building into a home. With that guiding principle, the team let the design and personality of each Madrigal dictate everything else.

In shaping each family member's character, design, and particularly their magical abilities, the art and story teams looked into the roles that existed within their own families and assigned powers that would organically speak to each one. "For example, we have the rock of the family who carries everyone's weight on their shoulders," says Jared Bush, "or the nurturing figure that could heal with their delicious cooking. This way, the powers assigned to each member didn't feel arbitrary, but were dictated by emotions and personality."

Once that piece was figured out, the visual development team applied it into their designs. The hair, facial features, physical appearance, and even costume details of each character were infused with elements of their magical power (or lack thereof). "A fun little detail is that we incorporated iconography specific to the powers of each family member onto their costumes. For example, Pepa has raindrops running down her dress and Bruno has hour glasses on his poncho. For contrast, the non-magical characters don't have that," said Ian Gooding.

Likewise, the house itself reflects the family and its collective personality: colorful, whimsical, fun, and imperfect. Almost like a teenager might decorate with band posters and school photos, the Madrigal rooms reflect the magical power and personality of their inhabitants—rock caves filled with sand and mysterious carvings for the one that can see the future, or a biodiverse rainforest for the one that can communicate with animals—and infuse the house with their many complex and clashing personalities of its inhabitants.

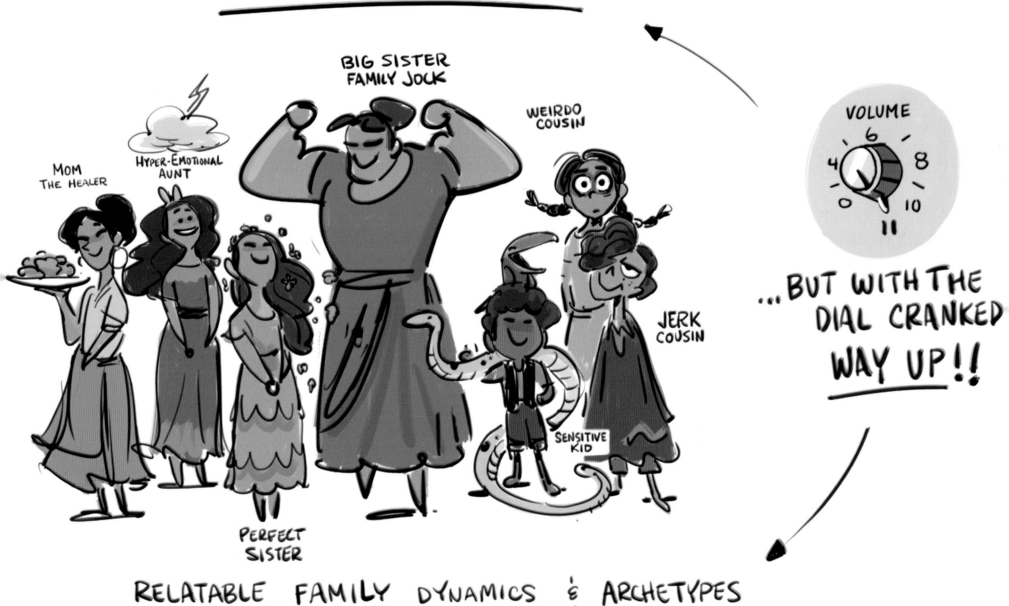

JUST LIKE EVERY FAMILY

BIG SISTER
FAMILY JOCK

WEIRDO
COUSIN

MOM
THE HEALER

HYPER-EMOTIONAL
AUNT

JERK
COUSIN

SENSITIVE
KID

PERFECT
SISTER

VOLUME

...BUT WITH THE
DIAL CRANKED
WAY UP!!

RELATABLE FAMILY DYNAMICS & ARCHETYPES

Abuela young   Abuela   Julieta   Agustin   Isabella   Luisa   Mirabel   Abuelo young

pantone 59-4C   pantone 44-2C   pantone 58-5   pantone 321-6C   pantone 51-5c   pantone 45-2C   pantone 321-6C

Dolores   Felix   Antonio   Pepa   Bruno   Camilo

one 67-4C   pantone 322-   pantone 4625 C   pantone 75-7C   pantone 52-5C   pantone 67-4C

One breakthrough the film team made in finding creative ways to show personality and family ties was through the use of color, as explained by Production Designers Ian Gooding and Lorelay Bové: "We assigned a different color palette to each branch of the family tree, to subtly cue to the audience who was related to whom. Mirabel's side of the family wears cool tones of blues, purples, and greens, while Pepa's side wears warm tones of orange, yellow, and red inspired by Félix's joyful Caribbean heritage. Abuela sits in the middle, dressed in darker shades of purple, brown, and black. The townspeople, on the other hand, wear neutral colors so the core family stands out with their vibrant hues."

THIS SPREAD: Lorelay Bové / Digital

ABUELA'S MIRACLE

THROUGHOUT LATIN AMERICA, there are many cultural ideas alluding to magic existing among ordinary things. One of those is the notion of "Encantos," places in nature filled with enchantment. "In Colombia, we are surrounded by sacred lands that feel magical, and we coexist with them, not questioning their existence," says guide Alejandra Espinosa. With this in mind, the filmmakers crafted the idea of a house and town that magically emerges from the earth as the response to a prayer made in a moment of desperation.

This sense of magic often comes from pain in Colombian magical realist literature. "I knew that many people from Colombia and Latin America identify with the idea of being displaced from their home town, so telling that tale with aspects of magical realism felt right for Abuela Alma's backstory. The land grants her a miracle when she begs for a way to escape the violence," says Co-Director Charise Castro Smith.

THIS SPREAD: **Matthias Lechner** / Digital

El Encanto

Bill Schwab / Digital

Mehrdad Isvandi / Digital

Ian Gooding / Digital

David Goetz / Digital

Ian Gooding / Digital

Mehrdad Isvandi / Digital

33

Matthias Lechner / Digital

Nancy Kruse / Digital

THE WORLD of ENCANTO

AN EDEN-LIKE PROTECTED VALLEY WHERE THE MADRIGAL FAMILY AND A SMALL VILLAGE LIVE

MOUNTAINS WERE MAGICALLY PUSHED UP TO CREATE THE PROTECTED VALLEY

THE VALLEY WAS CREATED WHEN A MIRACLE SAVED ABUELA ALMA & VILLAGERS

Jason Hand / Digital

"In Barichara some people told us stories of magic—we heard about a person walking in a secret forest and seeing a glowing light that led them to a talking snake, the guardian of this freshwater well. These stories were told in a way that is very matter of fact, where magic is normal and real."
—Jared Bush, Director

Mehrdad Isvandi / Digital

SOMETHING AROUND 140 FEET TALL
Mehrdad Isvandi / Digital

"The filmmakers were inspired by the Cocora Valley, which lies in the heart of the Andes mountains in Colombia. It is known for the wax palms—the tallest palm trees that we know of today—that grow in this region. This is also known as the coffee region, and it is surrounded by cloud forests that are usually very misty and magical."
—Felipe Zapata, Professor of Plant Biology

David Goetz / Digital

Scott Watanabe / Digital

Scott Watanabe / Digital

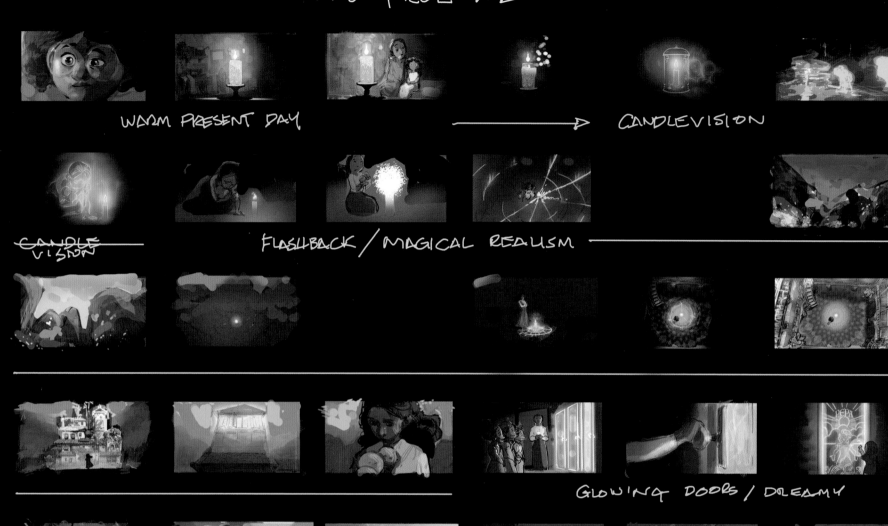

SEQ 100 PROLOGUE

WARM PRESENT DAY ———————————▷ CANDLEVISION

~~CANDLE VISION~~   FLASHBACK / MAGICAL REALISM

GREEN TINT SKY (CON'T)

GREEN TINT SKY (CON'T)

GLOWING DOORS / DREAMY

LAST FRAME → OF GOLDEN SKY

ENCANTO REVEAL

SEGUE BACK TO ABUELA / MIRABEL NINA

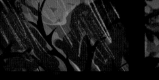

Manuel Arenas / Digital

"I collaborated with the lighting and art team to land on this idea of having mostly a single source of light here: the candle. It stays that way for most of the sequence, but there is also this colorful light explosion when the full Encanto is revealed, to accentuate that moment."
—Dan Cooper, Color and Lighting Lead

Jose F. Martinez / Digital

Abuela Alma

Jason Hand / Digital

Bill Schwab / Digital

Bill Schwab / Digital

Lorelay Bové / Digital

Abuela Awila

"Since the beginning, Abuela was always this stern, complicated person; someone that has to always look out for the well-being of her family and the town, with this painful connection to the past. There's a complexity to someone who always has to be hard, but also carries a deep vulnerability. I love the mix of the strong and the soft. To walk that line, we found a very warm beauty in her eyes, which comes from her younger self still living somewhere inside of her." —Bill Schwab, Art Director, Characters

Meg Park / Digital

Jin Kim / Digital

Bill Schwab / Digital

Bill Schwab / Digital

3. Black Lace Design

Design on shawl
Jaquard fabric

2.

3.

4. Skirt Trim design

Lorelay Bové / Digital

Lorelay Bové / Digital

"Because the house was an extension of Abuela at one point, rather than the whole family, the color of the wallpaper would reflect her mood in whatever room she was in. We explored what we could do with magical realism through human emotions."
—Lorelay Bové, Associate Production Designer

Casita

"Traditional Colombian architecture is abundant and beautiful, and earth is an important component while building typical homes. There are several variants: In one you have mud stucco walls called bahareque, which are made out of frames of organic materials like bamboo, filled with soil, and then plastered. Another is adobe, uncooked mud bricks, or tapia pisada that consists in a hollow structure with compressed layers of mud. For the roofs, it is common to use ceramic tiles called *tejas*."
—AGRA, Martin and Stefano Anzellini, Maria Inés Garcia-Reyes, Architects

Mehrdad Isvandi / Digital

Mehrdad Isvandi / Digital

IN THE DEVELOPMENT OF *Encanto*'s story, the house became not only a place but also a character. Early on, the filmmakers landed on the idea of the physical house as a literal representation of the family and their emotional connections. If the family is happy, the house is healthy, but if the family is going through struggles, the house too will crack.

"Both Byron and I naturally started to talk about the house as a character and about how fun it would be for it to just come alive. We knew early on that we didn't want to do a journey movie, so we wanted their home to be the most interesting place for everything to happen. At the same time, we wanted to show the diversity of environments in Colombia, so being able to have these endless magical rooms with different regions represented allowed us to do both," says Jared Bush.

With that in mind, just like the other characters of the Madrigal family, the magic and personality of the house itself needed to be translated into its visual design. Part of the team's challenge was taking that story-driven creative license and marrying it to traditional practices. "One way in which we brought in elements of traditional Colombian architecture was through the use of wooden beams used on the ceilings. There is a lot of thought that goes into this type of design, so we really had to study the way they built houses and talk to architects from the region," says Art Director, Environments Mehrdad Isvandi.

Jason Hand / Digital

Scott Watanabe / Digital

"Bringing the house to life and making it a character in the film is what I love about animation. We can do that. And while the house as a character allows for comedy, it also allows for emotion. Ultimately, the house represents the family and over the course of the film, as the family starts to have cracks, so does the house. And if we have done our job right, the audience will fall in love with the house and feel the pain when it falls." —Clark Spencer, Producer

Manuel Arenas / Digital

Mehrdad Isvandi / Digital

44

DOORS AND GIFTS

BEFORE

SWIRLS AS IT FORMS

AS A MADRIGAL CHILD NEARS THEIR 5TH BIRTHDAY A SWIRLY, GLOWING DOOR BEGINS TO FORM IN THE HOUSE.

AFTER

FORMS A DESIGN DEPICTING EACH CHILD'S UNIQUE GIFT

DESIGN & GLOW REMAIN AS A VISUAL REMINDER OF SPECIALNESS

ON THEIR 5TH BIRTHDAY WHEN THEY TOUCH THE DOORKNOB THEIR MAGICAL GIFT IS BESTOWED.

INSIDE MAGIC ROOMS

IT'S A JUNGLE IN THERE!

- THE ROOMS FORM IN THE MOMENT EACH MAGICAL CHILD TOUCHES THE DOORKNOB AND DISCOVERS THEIR GIFT.

- ROOMS AMPLIFY EACH CHILD'S GIFT BY CREATING A SPACE DESIGNED TO ALLOW EACH TO LEARN, PRACTICE, & GROW THEIR GIFT.

- VAST MAGICAL SPACES THAT ARE LARGER BY FAR THAN THE EXTERIOR BUILDING COULD HOLD.

THE HOUSE MOVEMENT

YES!

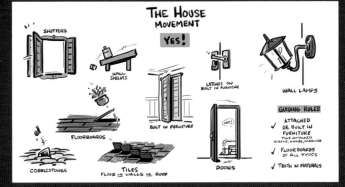

SHUTTERS

WALL SHELVES

LATCHES ON BUILT IN FURNITURE

WALL LAMPS

FLOORBOARDS

COBBLESTONES

TILES
FLOOR OR WALLS OR ROOF

BUILT IN FURNITURE

DOORS

HEY!

GUIDING RULES

✓ ATTACHED OR BUILT IN FURNITURE
PLUS ATTACHED SCREWS, KNOBS, HARDWARE

✓ FLOOR BOARDS OF ALL TYPES

✓ TRUTH IN MATERIALS

THE HOUSE MOVEMENT

NOPE!

TRUTH IN MATERIALS! No RUBBER WOOD

ONLY MADRIGAL HOUSE IS MAGICAL

No FREE MOVING FURNITURE

HOUSE CAN'T MOVE PLANTS

GET OUTTA MY SUN!

NONE OF OTHER HOMES ARE MAGICAL

HEY! WE WANT MAGIC TOO!

Jason Hand / Digital

"The design of the house was driven by character and story. We wanted to have Abuela's room at the center and then everyone else around her, in birth order, as much as we could. Mirabel's room is mirroring Abuela's room, so they are connected in that way. The colors of each section also match the character they are representing." —Mehrdad Isvandi, Art Director, Environments

Armand Serrano / Digital

45

THIS SPREAD: **Matthias Lechner** / Digital

THIS SPREAD: **Ian Gooding** / Digital

"Initially, the directors thought the story of *Encanto* would take place over 100 years through multiple generations, so I created these six paintings of the house during different decades. Since the house is both an environment and a character, I thought it'd be fun to explore its life."
—Ian Gooding, Production Designer

A House of Magical Realism

"I've always been drawn to heightened worlds because it is just so much more interesting and fun to feel our daily struggles, questions, and dilemmas through enchantments, living houses, or magical candles. When you make a myth out of all our intrinsic human fights, it is a much more satisfying story to tell because we can somehow process and sense our emotions better when they are externalized that way."
—Charise Castro Smith, Co-Director

Ian Gooding / Digital

THIS SPREAD: **Lorelay Bové** / Digital

Meg Park / Digital

Casita is Alive

Hillary Bradfield / Digital

Samantha Vilfort / Digital

Zane Yarbrough / Digital

Zane Yarbrough / Digital

Byron Howard / Digital

Dan Abraham / Digital

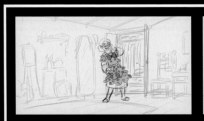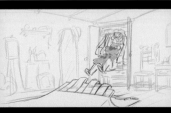

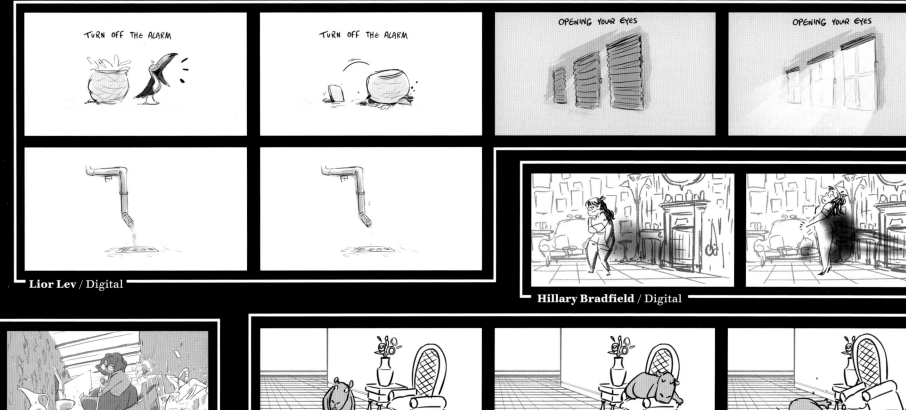

TURN OFF THE ALARM

TURN OFF THE ALARM

OPENING YOUR EYES

OPENING YOUR EYES

Lior Lev / Digital

Hillary Bradfield / Digital

Zane Yarbrough / Digital

Dan Abraham / Digital

As you would expect, the house was an exceptionally good listener.

It seemed to know when I needed to talk, and would create a little balcony, or a safe, cozy room where I could pour my heart out.

As I grew up, the magical building became my most trusted friend. And of all the family, I think I loved the house the most.

Byron Howard / Digital

"HUMILIATING"

IT'S ACTUALLY QUITE FUNNY IF YOU THINK ABOUT IT

ALWAYS LOOK ON THE BRIGHT SIDE OF LIFE

Tom Ellery / Digital

Zane Yarbrough / Digital

Ian Gooding / Digital

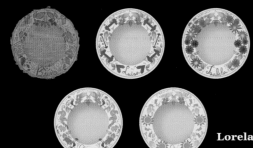

Lorelay Bové
/ Digital

"Designing the kitchen was all about making the space feel homey and unique. We added some curves and made things bulkier and thicker. Also, to add character into the space, I was able to leverage beautiful Colombian tilework. The kitchen includes artwork depicting the traditional black pottery from the La Chamba Community." —Mac George, Visual Development Artist

Mac George / Digital

Various Artists / Digital

Mac George / Digital

Mac George / Digital

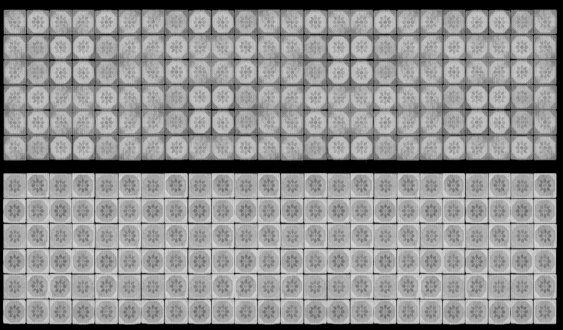

Lorelay Bové / Digital

Lorelay Bové / Digital

"We wanted to keep the courtyard symmetrical and have the rooms around it, as in real Colombian houses. It was important to have them on the same level, the second floor, to show that everyone is equal and there isn't a hierarchy." —Mehrdad Isvandi, Art Director, Environments

Mehrdad Isvandi / Digital

Mehrdad Isvandi / Digital

61

Lorelay Bové / Digital

"Every time we opened the door to a room, we asked the question: Should it feel like we just walked into a completely different dimension or should it feel like a part of the house, with an architectural component? We decided to have it feel like a real room that transitions into a magical but finite space."
—Mehrdad Isvandi, Art Director, Environments

Scott Watanabe / Digital

Scott Watanabe / Digital

Scott Watanabe / Digital

Matthias Lechner / Digital

Lorelay Bové / Digital

David Goetz / Digital

Matthias Lechner / Digital

THIS SPREAD: **Lorelay Bové** / Digital

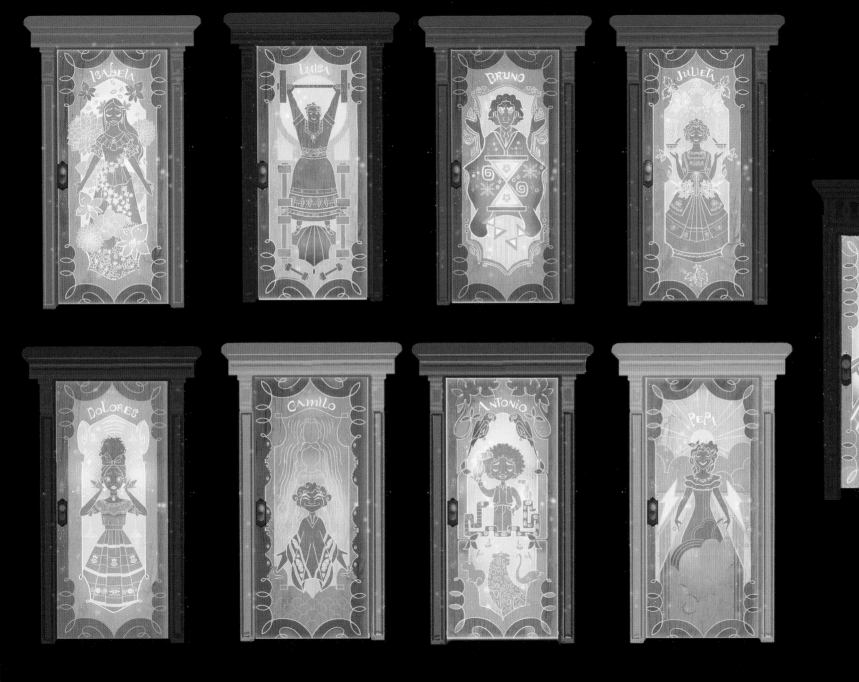

MIRABEL AND HER FAMILY

"THE MAIN REASON WHY I WAS ATTRACTED to telling this story was Mirabel," says Co-Director Charise Castro Smith. "I immediately went back to being an awkward preteen who was bullied, had wild curly hair, and had an awkward desperation to be a part of something. It felt really visceral and powerful to me, and I think a lot of people will relate to Mirabel as much as I did. We see her struggle, joy, triumph, and it is all earned coming from someone leading with their heart."

As the story of the Madrigals and their magical home began to take shape, it was led front and center by Mirabel, the one Madrigal born without powers. Her feelings of isolation and her relationship with her magical family members drove the story forward, as the writers and story artists explored her motivations and her flaws. "In an earlier version of the story, she was desperately trying to find a magical gift of her own, but it became apparent very quickly that she had likely grown past that desire already. For most of the film, she has accepted that she doesn't have a gift and she just wants to make her family proud despite that difference. This element of her motivation, wanting to be seen, felt much more relatable than a quest to find a magical power and ultimately shaped the story and relationships of *Encanto*," says Jared Bush.

THIS SPREAD: **Lorelay Bové** / Digital

Mirabel

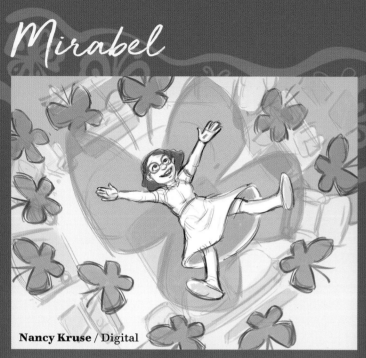

Nancy Kruse / Digital

Byron Howard / Digital

Lorelay Bové / Digital

Bill Schwab,
Lorelay Bové,
Meg Park, Jin
Kim, Camille
Andre, and Zane
Yarbrough /
Pencil, Digital

"This collection of images is called a blush-board. Ever since working on *Frozen*, I like to capture artwork that informs where we go in a single place. As the movie progresses, it is nice to have these boards hanging in the story rooms, to keep people excited and remind them of initial inspirations." —Bill Schwab, Art Director, Characters

Meg Park / Digital

Meg Park / Digital

Meg Park / Digital

Meg Park / Digital

Bill Schwab / Digital

Bill Schwab / Digital

"I now tend to forget that Mirabel is not a real person. I believe that she exists out there somewhere; she is not just a design we all approved, she is this living, breathing young woman who exists somewhere with her family."

—Byron Howard, Director

Dan Cooper / Digital

Jason Hand / Digital

Jason Hand / Digital

Bill Schwab / Digital

Lorelay Bové / Digital

Mirabel

"At one point during development, we thought about playing with the colors in the world around Mirabel, to reflect how her point of view is influenced by her emotions. In the third act of that version of the movie, Mirabel would stop narrating and the ending would be from Abuela's point of view, where everything would look more realistic and photographic. In the end, this idea was deemed to be a bit too distracting, but it was a fun experiment."
—Lorelay Bové,
Associate Production Designer

THIS SPREAD: **Lorelay Bové** / Digital

"Mirabel's clothing has a do-it-yourself aesthetic, which is meant to reflect her personality and scream: 'This is me!' It has a simple base that she has embroidered on top of, from the blouse to the skirt to her bag and shoes. Every element has been customized by hand. Mirabel's bag was inspired by the Mochila from the Wayuu Indigenous Community."—Neysa Bové, Costume Design Lead

4.E

"Makeover" before A.

"torn" after B.

Neysa Bové / Digital

Neysa Bové / Digital

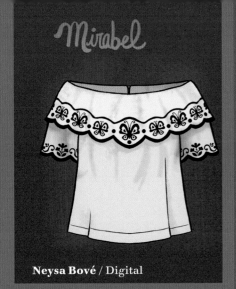

Mirabel

Neysa Bové / Digital

Neysa Bové / Digital

Neysa Bové / Digital

"We walked the team through the different regional outfits. Costumes from the Andean region were specifically important because that is where the film takes place. In this region during the late 19th and early 20th centuries, women would usually wear a white blouse with embroidery, a long skirt, and its corresponding petticoat. They would also wear shoes that are typical in Colombia called alpargatas (espadrilles) made from fique."
—Andrés Góngora and Sara Zamora, Anthropologists

Various Artists / Digital

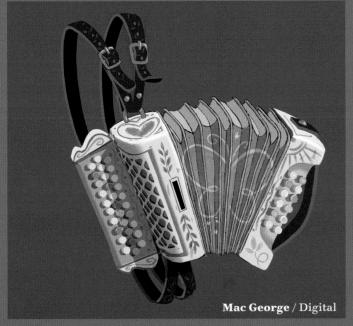

Mac George / Digital

Neysa Bové / Digital

shorter-band is "2 inches" above knee

THIS SPREAD: Neysa Bové / Digital

"Mirabel took a classic Colombian-inspired skirt that is wide and open, allowing a lot of movement, and then embroidered the heck out of it. Think of it as the scrapbook of a teenage girl. She has different icons to represent each member of her family: a basket of buñuelos for her mother, a chameleon for Camilo, flowers for Isabela. It really is a way to celebrate her family, because she is so proud of them. At the same time, she also wants people to see her, so there are loud elements like the pink tassels. It is imperfect and meant to feel handmade."
—Neysa Bové, Costume Design Lead

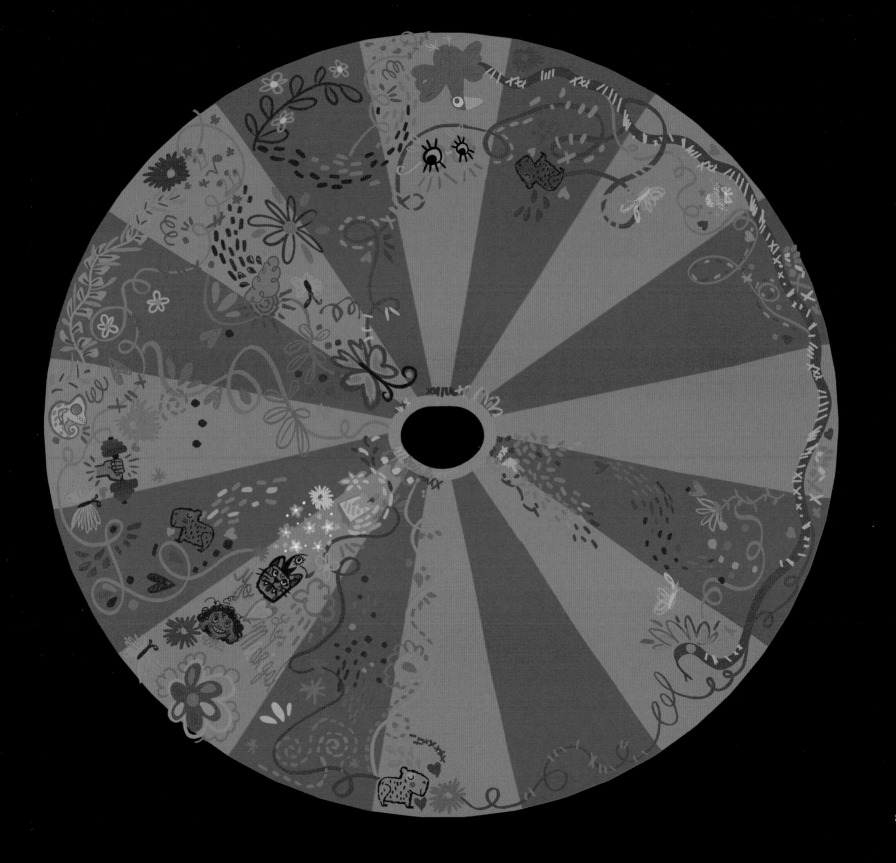

Lorelay Bové / Digital

Lorelay Bové / Digital

Mac George / Digital

"For this room, we wanted to convey Mirabel's personality, so it is full of quirky little objects like the doll and the little clay house maquette that is common in Colombia. The wallpaper is inspired by the animals of Colombia, and the wax palms are common to the area where the film is set. I also love the small details we tried to emphasize in her little workshop corner, where she made her clothes and crafts."
—Mac George, Visual Development Artist

Mirabel's Song

Byron Howard / Digital

Reprise

Jason Hand / Digital

"These are earlier versions of Mirabel's musical moments that Byron boarded for the main song and I boarded for a reprise. For the reprise, I wanted Mirabel to have a very magical moment, and having the house move the tiles around her was one way to do that. I started researching how the house could communicate this way, taking inspiration from videos of dominos falling and how they flipped to the other side." —Jason Hand, Head of Story

Mirabel's Color Keys

I am home

I am hurting....

Everyone has their own door.....

All I need is a moment to define myself

in my own way

And I just need a moment

THIS SPREAD: Lorelay Bové / Digital

Where is my moment

but I'm invisible in these hallways...

or a week or a day or a quarter hour...

I don't need a power...

"This was an earlier version of the song in which we played a lot with light. For example, the moment when they take a family picture, everything is overexposed from the camera's flash. Another opportunity to enhance the use of light was by having Mirabel dance around, using the sparklers to create butterfly wings."
—Lorelay Bové, Associate Production Designer

just a moment so you can know me........

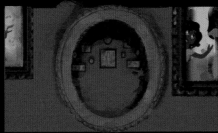

If only you could grow me a gift

"My sisters have always been (and still are) such an important part of my life—we have been through everything together. Seeing Isabela, Luisa, and Mirabel in this film reminds me so much of my own sisters. In *Encanto*, we wanted to explore some of the intricacies of sisterhood and show that even though it is not always an easy relationship, it is a very special one."
—Yvett Merino, Producer

Byron Howard / Digital

Zane Yarbrough / Digital

Lorelay Bové / Digital

88

Lorelay Bové / Digital

Luisa

"She was one of my favorite characters to design. We looked at a lot of female Olympic athletes, mostly hammer and shot-put throwers. I like that she has a soft feminine side to her, playing with the balance of a strong figure."

—Meg Park, Visual Development Artist

Bill Schwab / Digital

Meg Park / Digital

Jason Hand / Colored Pencil, Ink

Lorelay Bové / Digital

Bill Schwab / Digital

"I love Luisa because I enjoy characters I can push with exaggerated expressions and movement, and when I can laugh and experience crazy life events alongside them. Her song sequence is so different, complex but fun. I was so inspired by the work of the story artists, and I drew her with their work in mind."
—Jin Kim, Visual Development Artist

Jin Kim / Pencil, Digital

Jin Kim / Pencil, Digital

Meg Park / Digital

Bill Schwab / Digital

Bill Schwab / Digital

Jin Kim / Pencil, Digital

Neysa Bové / Digital

Neysa Bové / Digital

"For Luisa's costume, I noticed that many Colombian dance outfits had geometric shapes in them. So, I took that design aesthetic and added weights to represent her power. She wears bloomers under her skirt, which allow her to be physically active. We also tried an Olympic Victorian pantaloon-bloomer uniform from one of the first times women were included in the games." —Neysa Bové, Costume Design Lead

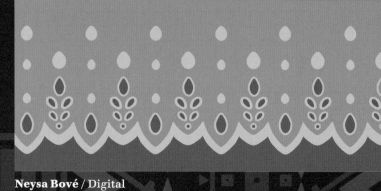

Neysa Bové / Digital

Griselda Sastrawinata-Lemay / Digital

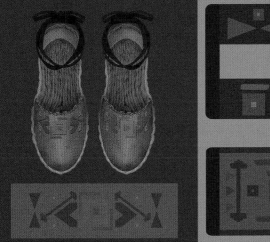

Neysa Bové / Digital

Matthias Lechner / Digital

Scott Watanabe / Digital

"We had many iterations of Luisa's room before it got cut completely from the film. At one point, Luisa had a very boring room, with everything made of stone to reflect that she had to be the responsible one. But she also had a secret exit to a hidden room that nobody knew about, with a theme park where she could just have fun like a little kid."
—Ian Gooding, Production Designer

Scott Watanabe / Digital

Scott Watanabe / Digital

Ian Gooding / Digital

Byron Howard / Digital

Luisa's Song

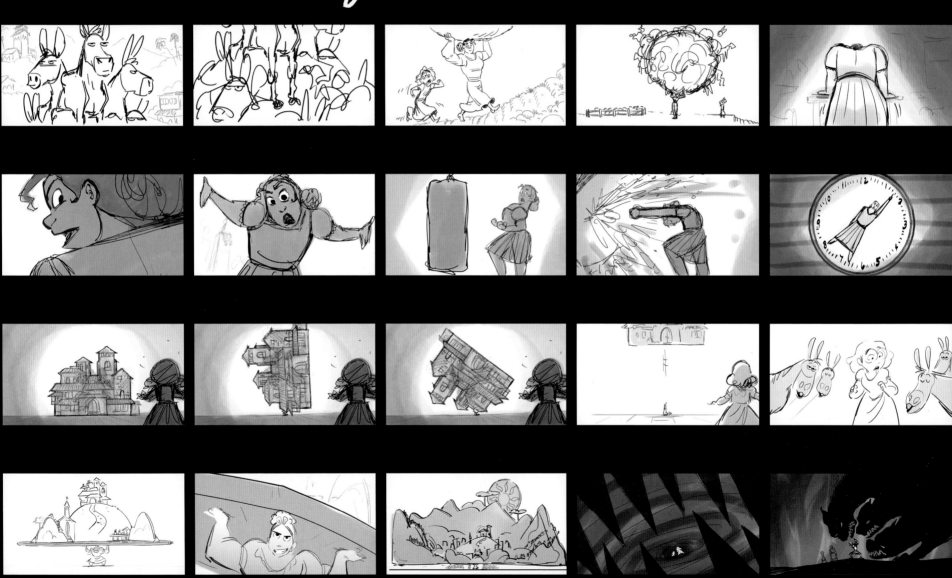

**THIS SPREAD: Tom Ellery, Mark Kennedy, Lior Lev,
and David VanTuyle** / Digital

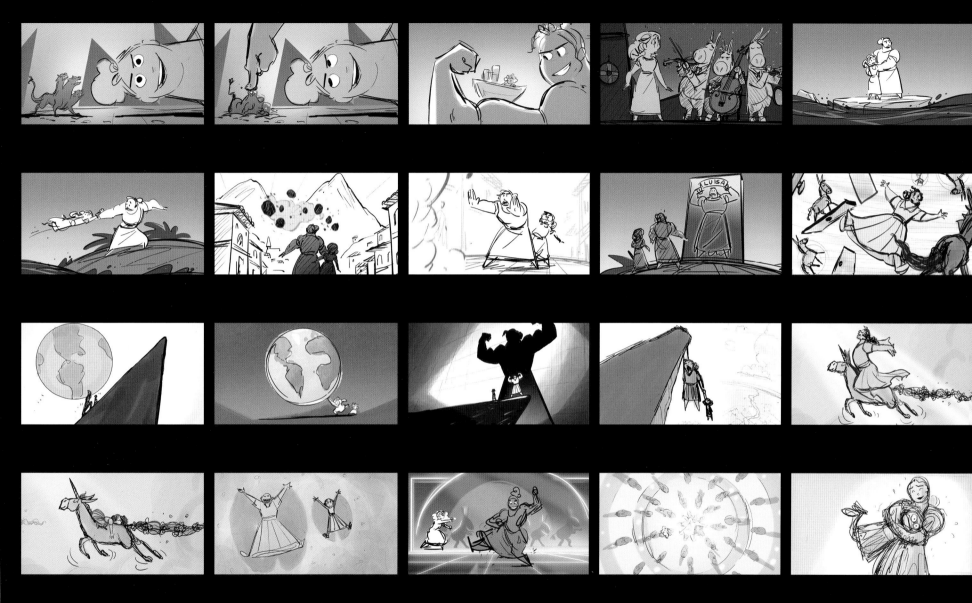

"In the first screening of *Encanto*, early in development, there was no song yet for this section. So instead of having a placeholder card that said 'Insert song here,' Jared had Luisa narrate the piece with this big, over-the-top dialogue and fun fantastical elements, and had me play with it visually. I knew it wasn't going to be in the final version, but it helped set the fun tone that we ended up with." —Tom Ellery, Story Artist

Luisa's Color Keys

THIS SPREAD: Lorelay Bové / Digital

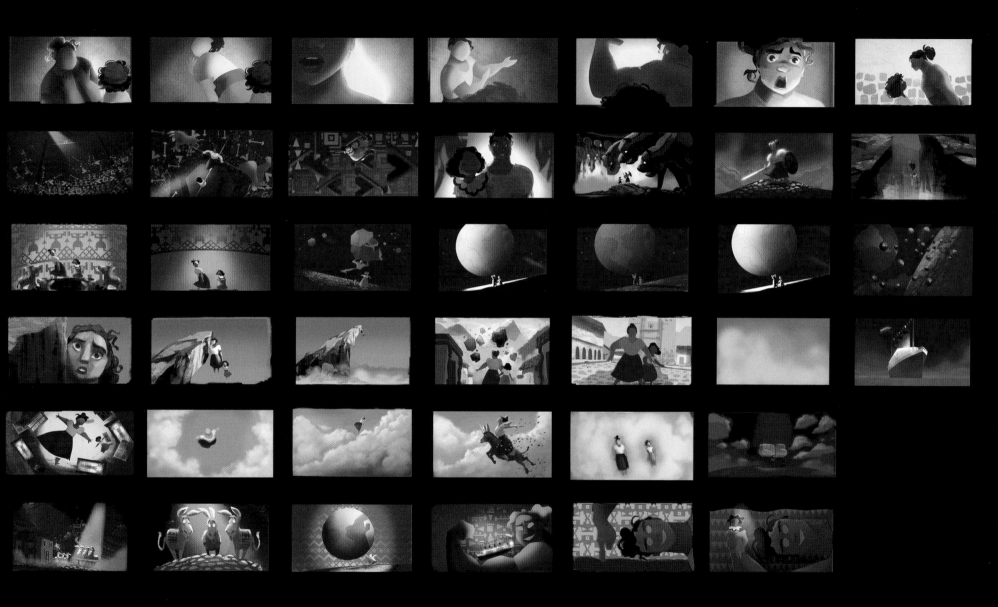

"For Luisa's song, I had fun making it more abstract than the rest of the film. It is so simple in aesthetic that it is easier to reflect her emotions through colors. For example, yellow represents gold, which shows the facade of her toughness. You can see a hint of the colors of the Colombian flag in there as well." —Lorelay Bové, Associate Production Designer

Isabela

"I knew Isabela was my favorite character from my first day on the film, when they showed me the visual development art. She's not rejecting femininity, she's not rejecting her gender expression, her makeup, or her dress; she's just becoming more of it on her own terms instead of having someone else tell her what it should be. To have someone break free like that is so powerful and inspiring." —Samantha Vilfort, Story Artist

Zane Yarbrough / Digital

Meg Park / Digital

Lorelay Bové / Digital

Bill Schwab / Digital

Lorelay Bové / Digital

Meg Park / Digital

Bill Schwab / Digital

Mi princesa!

Samantha Vilfort / Digital

Samantha Vilfort / Digital

Lorelay Bové / Digital

"She always had to look like this perfect golden child, but we wanted to incorporate this subtle undercurrent of anxiety at the same time, while she was trying so hard to portray the image of perfection for Abuela."
—Meg Park, Visual Development Artist

Meg Park / Digital

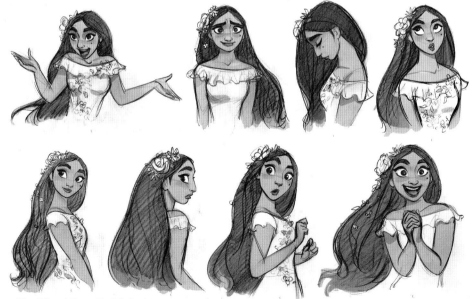

Jin Kim / Pencil, Digital

Bill Schwab / Digital

Bill Schwab / Digital

"Isabela is covered in flowers from head to toe. We chose the orchid embroidery around her neckline because it is the national flower of Colombia. She also wears a real orchid in her hair, and from the bust down she has all sorts of other Colombian flowers, like dahlias, made out of fabric. Everything is constructed in layers to look and feel like flower petals, inspired by her power." —Neysa Bové, Costume Design Lead

102 **Lorelay Bové** / Digital

Neysa Bové / Digital

Lorelay Bové / Digital

"Isabela's dress changes after her song. We explored many different iterations before landing on the final version in the film in which she is dressed in bolder colors, and we played with adding the flowers mentioned in the song to show her transformation."

—Lorelay Bové, Associate Production Designer

Neysa Bové / Digital

Neysa Bové / Digital

C.1   C.2   B.1   B.2   B.3

Everything in Isabela's room needed to feel like it was somehow related to flowers. We wanted the room to feel very intimate but be big enough for the song to happen in. After exploring different versions, we ultimately decided to have everything in pink and pastel colors, giving the vibe that she is princess-like. She later breaks free from this pressure, and her room becomes more colorful, expressive, and less constrained as a result. An example of elements that make her feel trapped are the curtains that surround her." —Camille Andre, Art Director, Environments

Camille Andre / Digital

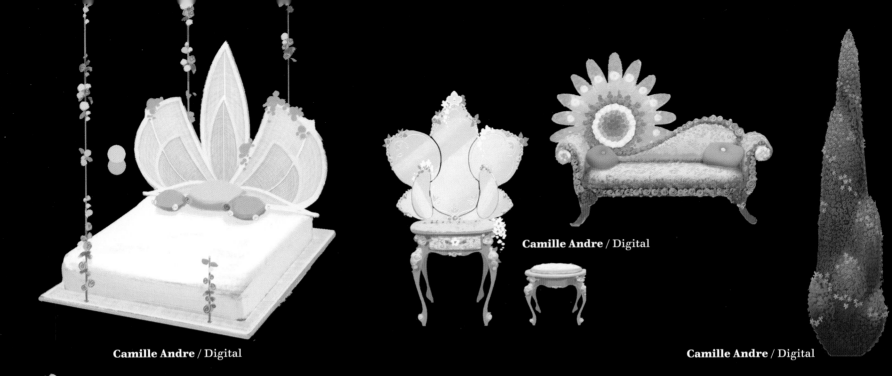

Camille Andre / Digital

Camille Andre / Digital

Camille Andre / Digital

Mehrdad Isvandi / Digital

Camille Andre / Digital

105

THIS SPREAD: **Lorelay Bové** / Digital

Isabela's Song

THIS SPREAD: Samantha Vilfort, Lior Lev, and **Nicole Mitchell** / Digital.

"Something that one of our consultants, Alejandra Espinosa, mentioned early on was that she hoped we would feature nature in a big way in this film, because that's a big source of pride for Colombians; and while many took it as inspiration for Antonio, I wanted to use it for Isabela through her flora powers, since Colombian flowers and plants are famous world-wide. She turns into this eclectic plant queen expressing every part of who she truly is." —Samantha Vilfort, Story Artist

Isabela's Color Keys

Julieta

"Other than Mirabel, Julieta is probably my favorite character. She reminds me of my own mom, and the relationship she has with Mirabel is very similar to the one I have with mine. She really tries, and her kids are her number one priority. She is the most empathetic member of the family, and while she is still imperfect, she tries her very best to defend her daughter." —Jared Bush, Director

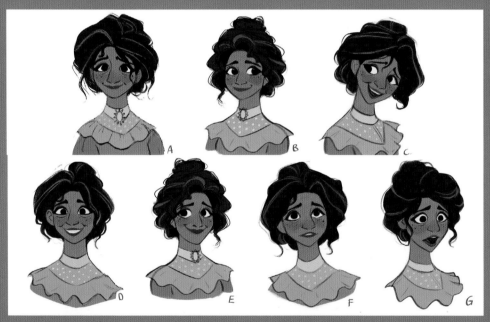

Meg Park / Digital

Byron Howard / Digital

Lorelay Bové / Digital

Meg Park / Digital

Griselda Sastrawinata-Lemay / Digital

Meg Park / Digital

Jin Kim / Digital   **Jin Kim** / Digital

"Julieta's power is healing, so I wanted to find iconography that symbolizes both healing and cooking. Herbs felt like the perfect balance of both, so I incorporated many Colombian-specific herbs on her outfit."

—Griselda Sastrawinata-Lemay, Visual Development Artist

Jin Kim / Digital   **Jin Kim** / Pencil, Digital   **Jin Kim** / Digital

Agustín

Meg Park / Digital

Bill Schwab / Digital

Byron Howard / Digital

"We always looked at Agustín as a city man, to expand on the origins of the family members. He is from somewhere similar to Bogotá, and he is very well put-together and wears a version of a three-piece suit, making him a fish out of water in this town."
—Bill Schwab, Art Director, Characters

Meg Park / Digital

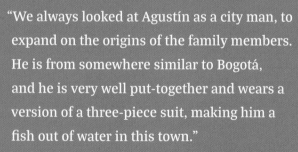

Griselda Sastrawinata-Lemay / Digital

Various Artists / Digital

Lorelay Bové / Digital

Jin Kim / Digital

"I wanted his outfit to complement Julieta's, because
I love making a good couple's costume. You can tell that
they belong together without being matchy-matchy. His
daughters are also present in his clothes: The flower in
his lapel is something Isabela gave him, and each one
of his socks represents his two other daughters, Mirabel
and Luisa."

—Griselda Sastrawinata-Lemay, Visual Development Artist

Nick Orsi / Digital

Jin Kim / Digital

Jin Kim / Digital

MIRABEL'S EXTENDED FAMILY

"I WANT PEOPLE TO FEEL LIKE THEY JUST SPENT time with a real family after watching the film," says Byron Howard. "I want them to picture what it is like to live with these people in this house and hopefully be completely immersed by it." This priority was front-and-center in making the character dynamics of *Encanto* feel relatable and real, the sort you might find in real extended families.

Many Walt Disney Animation Studios films focus on a single, central relationship between two characters. For *Encanto*, while Mirabel's emotional tie with Abuela is its core, the creative team wanted to try something different by having Mirabel experience a meaningful emotional bond with each one of her many family members. They also wanted Mirabel's family to include not only siblings and parents, but also cousins, aunts, and uncles, to reflect a multi-generational home that would ring true to many Latin American families. This was also an opportunity to show the ethnic diversity that can exist within families in Colombia.

With that in mind, they created a core cast of twelve, a group that would definitely fill up the family portrait. And since they didn't want the extended family members to act like fillers, the team purposely crafted each one to have a specific personality, look, and power. From the sweet and shy Antonio, to the loud Pepa, to the insecure Bruno, there are more than enough Madrigals to represent the classic familial roles that many will recognize in their own lives.

"I drew so many extended family members early on, even before we had a set story. I was inspired by the short stories Jared had written as exercises, in which everything was about magical realism and emotion. Through that exploration, we found the characters that you now see in the film."—Byron Howard, Director

Meg Park / Digital

Byron Howard / Digital

Byron Howard / Digital

Antonio

"Antonio starts the film with a white outfit because he still hasn't received his gift. After that happens, he changes into a more colorful version that incorporates the animals he can now communicate with. For that second costume, I was inspired by elements from the Caribbean coast outfits, like the red handkerchief." —Lorelay Bové, Associate Production Designer

Lorelay Bové / Digital

Lorelay Bové / Digital

Lorelay Bové / Digital

A17.5

A3

Jin Kim / Digital

Bill Schwab / Digital

Bill Schwab / Digital

Bill Schwab / Digital

Jason Hand / Digital

Jin Kim / Digital

Meg Park / Digital

"For Antonio, we explored many different facial features and hair tones. Our internal Walt Disney Animation Studios' Black Employees group was key to helping us find his final design, making him the beautiful little boy we have reflected in the film."
—Yvett Merino, Producer

Hyun Min Lee / Digital

Meg Park / Digital

123

"The rainforest from the Chocó region inspired Antonio's room. There are many different rainforests in South America, and we wanted it to feel specific to that region—we reviewed all the vegetation that exists in that area and made sure we were including the right plants."
—Mehrdad Isvandi, Art Director, Environments

Camille Andre / Digital

"We played with the idea of the room transforming from regular to magical, but decided to have it always remain in its magical form. However, we still wanted a transitional section before the bedroom becomes full-on rainforest, where the wallpaper goes from painting to real plants, and the tiles turn into moss."
—Camille Andre, Art Director, Environments

Camille Andre / Digital

Matthias Lechner / Digital

Scott Watanabe / Digital

David Goetz / Digital

Camille Andre / Digital

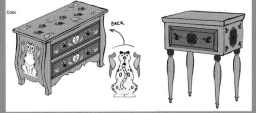

Camille Andre / Digital

Lorelay Bové / Digital

125

Jin Kim / Digital

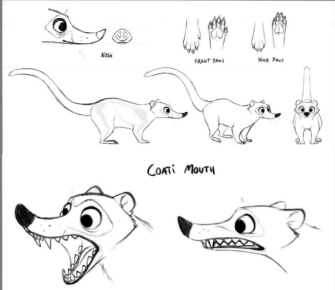

COATI MOUTH

Meg Park / Digital

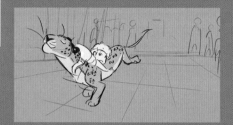

Samantha Vilfort / Digital

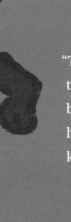

"The idea of having dozens and dozens of animals that love you, that you could hang out with—I would love that! In Colombia, the biodiversity is endless, so we could bring in chigüiros, tapirs, jaguars, hummingbirds, toucans, parrots, and many more. It felt like any kid's dream." —Jared Bush, Director

Bill Schwab / Digital

YOUR MARRIAGE IS A SHAM

Meg Park / Digital

Meg Park / Digital

"We wanted Antonio's animals to be beautiful and fun, while still feeling realistic. They might act slightly different around Antonio, but they don't talk or behave in human ways."
—Bill Schwab, Art Director, Characters

Jason Hand / Watercolor

Meg Park / Digital

Bill Schwab / Digital

Bill Schwab / Digital

Jin Kim / Digital

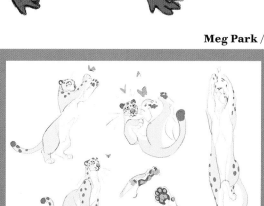

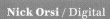

Nick Orsi / Digital

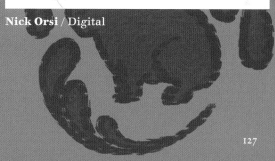

Nick Orsi / Digital

Dolores

"It was very important to get Dolores' hair right. I work with organizations that promote the use of natural hair, and it was something important for me to portray in the film, so I collaborated with the team to find the right look for her."

—Edna Liliana Valencia Murillo, Afro-Colombian Consultant

Bill Schwab / Digital

Brittney Lee / Digital

Jin Kim / Digital

Jason Hand / Digital

Meg Park / Digital

Dolores

Neysa Bové / Digital

Neysa Bové / Digital

Jin Kim / Digital

Jin Kim / Digital

"Imagine recasting an actor more than three times—that was my experience with all the costume changes for Dolores. We had to adapt and ended up with this beautiful take where you can see the influence of both her parents. Her father's Caribbean heritage comes through in her loose blouse and skirt with red highlights, inspired by the cumbia dress."
—Neysa Bové, Costume Design Lead

Camilo

Jason Hand / Digital

Jin Kim / Pencil, Digital

"Camilo early on was an angry teen, with his hair kind of covering one eye, messy, but he probably spends over an hour getting it to look like that and convey attitude. Griselda Sastrawinata-Lemay did the same for his design by having his poncho deliberately just off one shoulder."
—Bill Schwab, Art Director, Characters

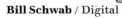

Bill Schwab / Digital

Meg Park / Digital

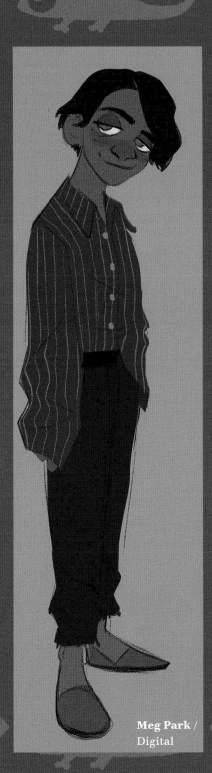

Meg Park / Digital

Griselda Sastrawinata-Lemay / Digital

"Camilo's iconography is a chameleon to reflect his shape-shifting power, and though it appears on the poncho and the weaving on his sandals, it is often hidden as a nod to him disguising himself."

—Griselda Sastrawinata-Lemay, Visual Development Artist

Bill Schwab / Digital

Pepa

Seth Boyden / Digital

Meg Park / Digital

Meg Park / Digital

Meg Park / Digital

"Initially, Pepa's power was to be indestructible, and she had this daredevil side to her, but it felt too similar to Luisa's strength. So we landed on the weather power for her, which made sense because she is the fun, strange aunt trying to keep it together."
—Meg Park, Visual Development Artist

Meg Park / Digital

Meg Park / Digital

Meg Park / Digital

"We designed a fusion of several folkloric dresses for Pepa from different regions, including Tolima, using classic elements like the puff sleeve. We also had to think about the functionality of the costume with her power, since she constantly has wind and rain around her. Her clothes include iconography that represents her powers too, like lightning bolts, raindrops, and little suns as earrings."
—Neysa Bové, Costume Design Lead

Neysa Bové / Digital

Camille Andre / Watercolor, Digital

David Goetz / Digital

Jin Kim / Pencil, Digital

Félix

Nick Orsi / Digital

"Agustín and Félix were originally explored as a double act. They were the outsiders, and they had a connection to Mirabel because they also don't have powers, in their case, because they married into the family."
—Meg Park, Visual Development Artist

Bill Schwab / Digital

Bill Schwab / Digital

Bill Schwab / Digital

Bill Schwab / Digital

Samantha Vilfort / Digital

> we just have that spark!

Griselda Sastrawinata-Lemay / Digital

Felix -- Shirt detail

shirt color   trim color

Griselda Sastrawinata-Lemay / Digital

Collar graphic design

color

embroidery direction

Button

cotton thread
cotton embroidery thread
Wood

color

Ribbon detail

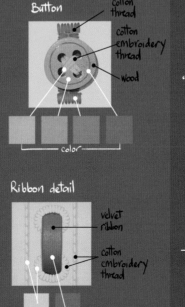

velvet ribbon
cotton embroidery thread

"His costume is meant to reflect his personality and who he is. He is very sweet and supportive of his wife and kids, so the geometric shapes in his costume, like the triangle, represent that stability he gives them. His shirt is a traditional guayabera, which is very common in the Colombian Caribbean Coast, the region that inspired his character."

—Griselda Sastrawinata-Lemay, Visual Development Artist

Living with Extended Family

Jason Hand / Digital

Jason Hand / Digital

Mark Kennedy / Digital

Ryan Green / Digital

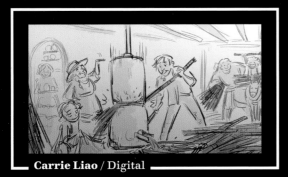

Carrie Liao / Digital

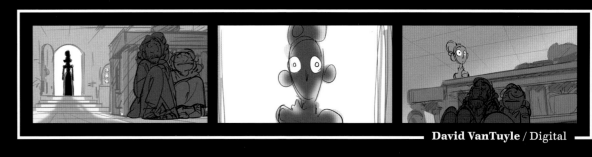

David VanTuyle / Digital

Carrie Liao / Digital

David VanTuyle / Digital

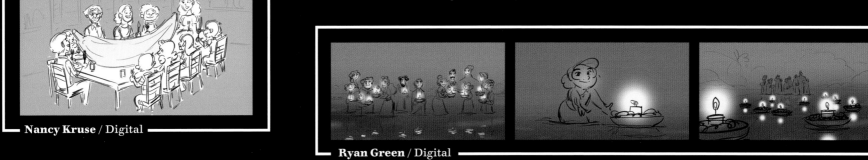

Ryan Green / Digital

Nancy Kruse / Digital

Zane Yarbrough / Digital

Bruno

"His costume is meant to be the old ceremonial outfit that he used to wear when he was having visions of the future for the people that came to see him. He has had it for a long time, and it is now an old, sad version of what it once was."

—Meg Park, Visual Development Artist

Meg Park / Digital

Meg Park / Digital

Meg Park / Digital

Meg Park / Digital

Jin Kim / Digital

James Woods / Digital

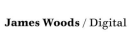

Nick Orsi / Digital

Jin Kim / Digital

Meg Park / Digital

PONCHO WITH PATTERN   WOVEN FABRIC BASE   BACK   HOOD

PRINT EXTENDS DOWN THE REVERSE SIDE

Meg Park / Digital

Lorelay Bové / Digital

Byron Howard / Digital

"For Bruno, I did a ton of research into people who are confined and don't have human communication. I thought about what it would be like for Bruno to be burdened with this gift of being able to see the future—how would that affect his personality? How are people affected when they're shunned by their families?" —Mark Kennedy, Story Artist

Jin Kim / Digital

Bill Schwab / Digital

Bill Schwab / Digital

Bill Schwab / Digital

Camille Andre / Digital

Camille Andre / Digital

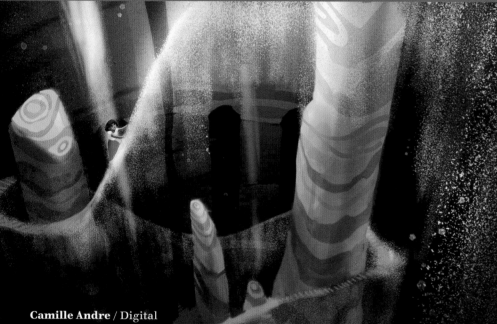

Camille Andre / Digital

"It took a lot of exploration to find the look of this room. At first it was meant to feel more like a cave mixed with the architecture of a cathedral, and then it evolved into this mountain-inspired room. The finished design is inspired by the Estoraques, which are very special natural rock formations in Colombia."
—Camille Andre, Art Director, Environments

Camille Andre / Digital

Camille Andre / Digital

Mehrdad Isvandi / Digital

Mark Kennedy / Digital

Zac Retz / Digital

"There couldn't be normal furniture, so I had to make it up—for example, the shelves were made from an old suitcase. His chair is a broken version of the same ones they have in the house, and his little table looks into the dining room, as if he were somehow a part of the family dinners from afar." —Mac George, Visual Development Artist

Jose F. Martinez / Digital

Mac George / Digital

Camille Andre / Digital

Mac George / Digital

MIRABEL'S COMMUNITY

"BYRON AND I TALKED ABOUT HOW COOL it would be if people could talk about the town as if it were a real place that actually existed in Colombia," says Jared Bush. "If people looked hard enough, they could find their way to it somehow. Early on, I even created a website for the town, to give us that sensation that it was indeed real as we were crafting the story."

While the Madrigal family is the main focus of *Encanto*, they are very much a part of their town and its people. The family has the responsibility to use their gifts for the good of their society, and Abuela always has to make sure that the magic is working properly, because the whole village depends on it. The people in the town come from different regions of Colombia, making the Encanto a place where they all came together and brought their specific cultures.

In designing the town itself, it was important to make sure that it reflected the warmth of the people and the music that lives in the streets of Colombia, and that the crowds represented Colombia's ethnic diversity. The creative team drew inspiration from towns such as Barichara and Salento, and the surrounding areas were inspired by another iconic Colombian location: the Cocora Valley, famous for its stunning wax palms.

THIS SPREAD: Ian Gooding / Digital

The Town

"The town square with the church at the center, designed by Dan Cooper, turned into our focal point, and we continued to build around it. We wanted the house to be nearby and not too elevated, so the family felt like a part of the community and not totally disconnected." —Mehrdad Isvandi, Art Director, Environments

Zac Retz / Digital

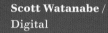

Scott Watanabe / Digital

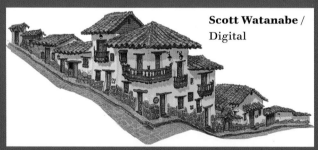

Scott Watanabe / Digital

Scott Watanabe / Digital

David Womersley / Digital   **David Womersley** / Digital

Photographs by **Byron Howard** and **Jared Bush**

Zac Retz / Digital

Zac Retz / Digital

"There was a point in the story's development when Abuela and Mirabel went to the city that Abuela was originally from. There, they would see vehicles, including the traditional Chiva bus, and technology that was not available in their hidden little town."

—Ian Gooding, Production Designer

Mac George / Digital

Zac Retz / Digital

Scott Watanabe / Digital

Dan Cooper / Digital

Scott Watanabe / Digital

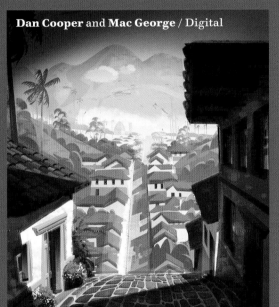

Dan Cooper and **Mac George** / Digital

Dan Cooper / Digital

David Goetz / Digital

The Townspeople

Jin Kim / Digital

"Designing crowd characters is sometimes more difficult than designing the main cast, because you have to walk the line of making them not stand out too much and steal attention, while making sure that they still have their own flavor."
—Jin Kim, Visual Development Artist

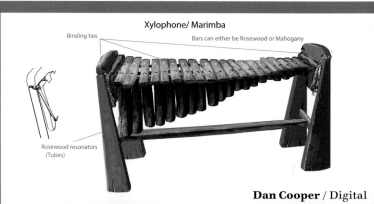

Xylophone/ Marimba

Binding ties

Bars can either be Rosewood or Mahogany

Rosewood resonators (Tubes)

Dan Cooper / Digital

Various Artists / Digital

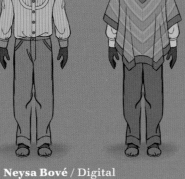

Neysa Bové / Digital

"For the villagers' costumes we kept basic silhouettes, wanting to make them look and feel like regular people you might see in the Colombian coffee region. Their palette is more neutral, so our Madrigal family could stand out. As part of the garments, we included depictions of the Sombrero Vueltiao from the Zenú Indigenous Community and the Sombrero Aguadeño from the Aguadas Community."
—Neysa Bové, Costume Design Lead

Neysa Bové / Digital

Neysa Bové / Digital

149

1. 2. 3. 4. 5. 6. 7.

Neysa Bové / Digital

Neysa Bové / Digital

Neysa Bové / Digital

150

Meg Park / Digital

Jin Kim / Digital

Jin Kim / Digital

Jin Kim / Digital

Jin Kim / Digital

Jin Kim / Digital

151

Mariano y Bubo

Meg Park / Digital

Meg Park / Digital

Meg Park / Digital

Meg Park / Digital

Ryan Green / Digital

Meg Park / Digital

Meg Park / Digital

"Mariano was so much fun to work on. The directors pitched him as this unbelievably good-looking, picture-perfect man, so I looked at a lot of different telenovela and Latino movie stars to inspire him. Neysa gave him an iteration of the crowd costumes, with a classic Colombian guayabera, to make him feel like a part of the town."
—Meg Park, Visual Development Artist

"At one point Isabela had a suitor named Bubo, that came from the city, with a much more modern look compared to the rest of the town. It was a really funny idea; he was a true fish out of water with a dorky personality." —Bill Schwab, Art Director, Characters

Bill Schwab / Digital

Bill Schwab / Digital

Bill Schwab / Digital

Jin Kim / Pencil, Digital

Meg Park / Digital

Samantha Vilfort / Digital

"In the end, Isabela's journey is not defined by a guy. She is her own woman, still finding herself. Samantha Vilfort created some beautiful early designs to show a more punk-rock version of who she originally was."
—Yvett Merino, Producer

THE NEW MIRACLE

Jin Kim / Digital

Jin Kim / Digital

"Ryan Tottle and I worked on early versions of Mirabel with the images provided by Visual Development. In this version, you can see a simpler anatomy, when we were looking at more stylized versions of the character. She is also wearing an earlier version of the costume with an oversized coat, which we explored for a while." —Sergi Caballer, Character Model Supervisor

THIS PAGE: Ryan Tottle and
Sergi Caballer / Digital

Bill Schwab and **Various Artists** / Digital

MAYBE KEEP WAIST AREA FAIRLY CLEAN, SO THE BULK OF MOVEMENT PIVOTS FROM HIPS?

Alex Kuperschmidt and **Various Artists** / Digital

"We go back and forth in the process; no design work is really linear. After the modelers finished a first pass based on our Mirabel sketches, they gave us a work-in-progress model and we would do draw-overs to continue evolving the character, adding to the anatomy and design. So even though Visual Development designs the characters initially, modelers like Ryan and Sergi have a big hand in finding the overall look." —Bill Schwab, Art Director, Characters

"The work evolved, and we started to land on the right balance between stylization and naturalism through the creation of Abuela Alma's model. Then we did the same for Mirabel and evolved the design closer to human anatomy. A good place to see this more naturalistic change is in the necklines. By this point we had received the final design of her outfit, and we really accentuated the shape of the skirt to give it a sense of folkloric Colombian costumes."
—Sergi Caballer, Character Model Supervisor

Sergi Caballer / Digital

"Rigging is putting a skeleton in a character and providing controls for the animators; it's like creating an armature for a puppet. For *Encanto*, we were able to add more facial and eyelash rigs, which really helped elevate a character like Mirabel who is so expressive."
—Jennifer Downs, Character Technical Director

Nicklas Puetz, Jennifer Downs, and **Various Artists** / Digital

"For the hair, Xinmin Zhao (Character Technical Director) and I went around the whole studio to find real-life references, to find the right type of curl that she has. Charise's curls were an inspiration. I don't know if she knows that! I also partnered with Mary Twohig, who was in charge of cloth simulation for such a challenging costume. " —Jose Luis "Weecho" Velasquez, Character Look Development Artist

Jose Luis "Weecho" Velasquez, Xinmin Zhao, and **Various Artists** / Digital

Jose Luis "Weecho" Velasquez, Mary Twohig, and **Various Artists** / Digital

"The Look Development Department takes what Modeling does and adds textures and materials. For Mirabel, I virtually stitched all the embroidery by hand, something I had never done before and had to learn. We studied many different types of yarn and how a creative teenage girl would do this." —Jose Luis "Weecho" Velasquez, Character Look Development Artist

Various Artists / Digital

Various Artists / Digital

"In animation, our primary focus is to build character performances that connect with the audience emotionally. Understanding what a character is feeling, and why they feel that way, is our guiding principle. Stephanie Beatriz provided nuance and depth as the voice of Mirabel, and we studied her characteristics and mannerisms in order to make Mirabel as unique as possible. We have also been fortunate to have a wide variety of Colombian artists and experts to help inform and create believable performances that will hopefully represent, and resonate with, the people of Colombia. The artists marry all this knowledge and research with their personal experiences and feelings to bring Mirabel to life on the screen."
—Kelly McClanahan, Animation Supervisor

The Fall of Casita

Seth Boyden / Digital

Seth Boyden / Digital

Camille Andre / Digital

"The family strikes a balance of what they think works for them, and when Mirabel starts rocking the boat and showing cracks in that balance, everyone tells her to stop. However, sometimes you have to destroy the boat in order to build a new one that can fit everyone, rather than excluding the people that don't fit."
—Nancy Kruse, Head of Story

UNITY OF FAMILY & HOUSE

FAMILY

HOUSE

THE FAMILY & HOUSE ARE TIED TOGETHER.
IF THE FAMILY HAS PROBLEMS SO DOES THE HOUSE.

Jason Hand / Digital

CRACKS

- VISUAL REPRESENTATION OF FAMILY PROBLEMS.

- A "SYMPTOM" OF THE FAMILY'S DYSFUNCTION SHOWN THROUGH HOUSE

LIKE A HOUSE WITH AN UNSTABLE FOUNDATION

I'M WILTING

LUISA DON'T LIKE CRACKS

THE FAMILY IS IN A UNHEALTHY STATE.

Camille Andre / Digital

Lorelay Bové / Digital

Lorelay Bové / Digital

Camille Andre / Digital

163

Lorelay Bové / Digital

Alma y Pedro

"In the younger version of Alma, we really explored the softer, more motherly part of her, before she became an iron-fisted lady through tragedy."
—Meg Park, Visual Development Artist

Jin Kim / Pencil, Digital

Meg Park / Digital

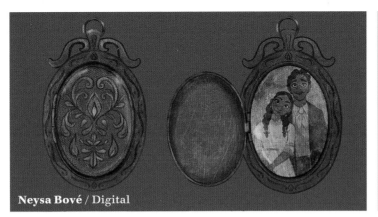

Neysa Bové / Digital

Lorelay Bové / Digital

"Pedro's personality came from the script and storyboards, so I translated that into the designs. He is a writer, so I wanted to give him that soul; he sits at his desk and writes poems."—Jin Kim, Visual Development Artist

Jin Kim / Pencil, Digital

Jin Kim / Pencil, Digital

Bill Schwab / Digital

Bill Schwab / Digital

Abuela's Song

THIS SPREAD: Byron Howard / Digital

Cinematography: Lighting and Layout

THIS SPREAD: **Various Artists** / CG Render

WITH THE CLEAR DIRECTIVE that the film was to be character-driven throughout the pipeline, the departments responsible for cinematography (Layout and Lighting) were no exception to this principle.

"For the cinematography of *Encanto*, we wanted to do something different," says Nathan Warner, Director of Cinematography, Layout. "We decided to have this film be the first Walt Disney Animation Studios production to use a tall frame since *Tangled*, which came out over ten years ago, because we wanted to be able to get closer to the characters. A wide frame is better suited for big action adventures, and this is such an intimate piece."

"To complement the intimacy that Layout is going for, in Lighting we landed on Romanticism, the philosophy of letting emotion lead design. The directors wanted to express strong emotions through the optics of the movie. This would also amplify, exaggerate, and distort perception, which is very in line with Mirabel's point of view as a narrator," explain Alessandro Jacomini and Daniel Rice, Directors of Cinematography, Lighting. "The candle has also been such a focal point for our work as a source of light, symbolizing togetherness and hope." Lighting also took Mirabel's sentiment of being left out and let it come through the emotional lighting style in her scenes.

The directors constantly reminded the team about the emotional subtext of each scene and the complexities of the individual moments. Warner, Jacomini, and Rice then implemented that subtext in complex sequences, such as Luisa's song, which is overall very comedic but has an emotional sophistication that comes through camera angles and lighting choices and accentuates the dramatic weight that Luisa carries. The moment in which Mirabel sits alone on her bed is also very emotionally complex, and the cinematography puts the audience right next to her, going through the same emotions as her.

The New Miracle

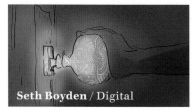

Seth Boyden / Digital

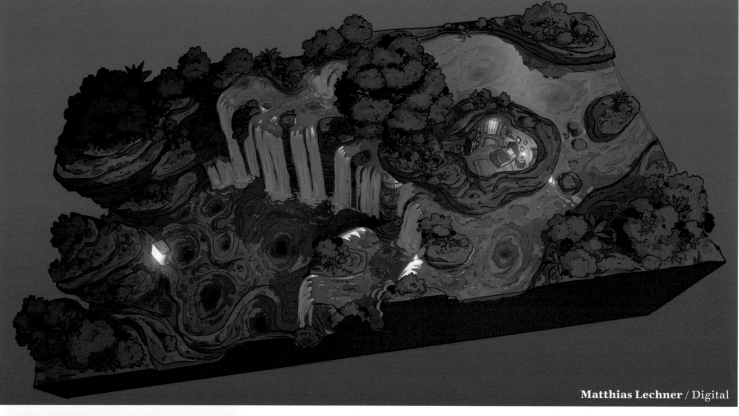

Matthias Lechner / Digital

Dan Cooper / Digital

Seth Boyden / Ink, Pencil

"Early in the development of the film, Byron and Jared talked about this idea that the house needed to fall–representing the fall of the family–and then be rebuilt in order for the Madrigals to be healed. The visuals and imagery of that spoke to me. Family is complicated. And when a family really opens up to each other and shares their truth, their real feelings, it is likely to get very messy, but on the other side of that messiness lies a stronger, more connected and loving family."
—Clark Spencer, Producer

Zac Retz, Meg Park / Digital

"We had so many different versions of the ending, and I can see the pieces of each that made it into the final one. It is a complex scene because we wanted to achieve many things: have a new version of the miracle that is now catalyzed by Mirabel, mirror the moment in which she didn't get her gift, fulfill Pedro's promise and Bruno's vision, and give a resolution to every family member's journey." —Seth Boyden, Story Artist

Zac Retz, Bill Schwab / Digital

Lorelay Bové / Digital

Bill Schwab / Digital

Lorelay Bové / Digital

Camille Andre / Digital

Camille Andre / Digital

Lorelay Bové / Digital

Acknowledgments

IT HAS BEEN A TRUE JOY to be able to follow the development and production of *Encanto* from start to finish, and to help the filmmakers tell the story of the art through this book. It truly feels as if I got to curate a museum exhibit with pieces from some of the finest artists in the animation industry. Thanks to Byron Howard, Jared Bush, Charise Castro Smith, Yvett Merino, and Clark Spencer for allowing me to be a partner in crafting this story.

Thanks to the fabulous Ian Gooding, Lorelay Bové, Bill Schwab, Camille Andre, Mehrdad Isvandi, Jason Hand, Nancy Kruse, and every artist that was a part of this journey. To our cultural team, Kalikolehua Hurley and Stephanie Lopez, and our key consultants, thanks for your partnership to sew Colombian culture into the fabric of this film. Heather Blodget, Ashley Lam, and Babatunde Akinloye, you were dream collaborators through this journey. Thanks to Jessica Julius for her mentorship throughout this process. Thank you to the Walt Disney Animation Studios' *Familia* group and Walt Disney Animation Studios' Black Employees group for their collaboration. Thank you to John McGuire and Christine Chrisman along with their legal team, and to Amy Astley and the Public Relations team, for their partnership throughout this process.

Thanks to the guidance of Alison Giordano and Jackson Kaplan from Disney Publishing; your thoughtfulness and kindness while collaborating on this piece were invaluable. Thanks to the team at Chronicle: Julia Patrick, Brittany McInerney, Juliette Capra, Neil Egan, Jon Glick, Alison Petersen, and Tera Killip. I have learned so much from your experience and work both in editing and design. It has been a true joy putting this book together alongside you all.

Finalmente, gracias a mi mamá, papá, hermanos, cuñados, sobrinos, suegros y familia extendida—sin ustedes ningún sueño sería posible. A mis ahijados Isabella y Rafael. A mis esposo, Chris Wahl, por darme alegría y amor en todo momento. Esta experiencia ha sido un verdadero encanto!

–Con Mucho Cariño,
JUAN PABLO REYES LANCASTER JONES

SIEMPRE HAY OTRA PUERTA

ENCANTO

Byron Howard / Digital

Renato dos Anjos / Pencil